The Galleria Borghese

Paul den Arend

Copyright © 2015 by Paul den Arend

All rights reserved. No part of this publication may be reproduced, distributed, or transmitted in any form or by any means, including photocopying, recording, or other electronic or mechanical methods, without the prior written permission of the publisher, except in the case of brief quotations embodied in critical reviews and certain other noncommercial uses permitted by copyright law.

Book design and production by VandiDesign
Editing by Paul den Arend

Published by: VandiDesign, Meerweg 112 9752 JL Haren, The Netherlands

DEDICATION

This book is dedicated to the many people that I have guided through the Galleria Borghese and the city of Rome.

CONTENTS

Map of the Galleria Borghese 2

Introduction 3

Part 1: Ground floor 10

Part 2: First Floor 51

Part 3: Background 72

Sources 93

Map of the Galleria Borghese
Ground Floor

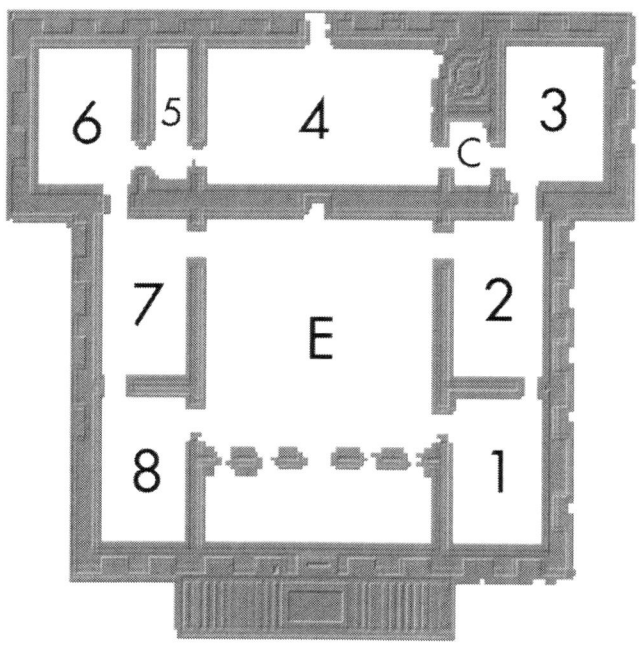

1. Room of Pauline
2. Room of David
3. Room of Apollo and Daphne
4. Room of the Emperors
5. Room of Hermaphrodite
6. Room of Aeneas
7. Egyptian Room
8. Room of the Faun

C: Chapel

E: Entrance Hall

The Galleria Borghese

Introduction

The Museum

The Galleria Borghese in Rome is in my opinion one of the most beautiful museums in the city (and in the world). It is a small museum with an exquisite collection, housed in a beautiful villa. Many of Gian Lorenzo Bernini's early works can be found here. If you are ever in Rome, make sure to visit it. In my experience, many people find this museum even more beautiful than the Vatican Museums, something they did not expect beforehand. This might also have something to do with the fact that the Galleria has a strict reservation system.

The museum only lets a certain amount of people in and once it's full, they close the doors. This makes a visit to the museum a really nice experience. It's nothing like the Vatican Museums, where the massive crowds can lower your enjoyment tremendously. If you would like to visit the museum, be sure to book your ticket beforehand on the internet. Without reservation it is impossible to get in. Often, the museum is sold out for the next two weeks, so make sure to plan ahead and book online.

This guidebook will tell you the stories of all the great art in the museum. I will show you which pieces are most famous and why. Many of these artworks have interesting stories behind them and it will be much more enjoyable looking at them when you know the story.

This book does not aspire to be a complete guide to all the artworks in the museum. I will show you the many highlights, but leave out the lesser known works. I will take you on a tour through the museums, just like I would take a tour group.

I have guided many groups through the museum and I always find it an enormous pleasure to be able to show people the many artworks that I love. The Galleria is one of my favorite places to show people around and I hope you will find your visit as enjoyable as I always enjoy mine.

Bernini

Many of the most important sculptures in the Galleria Borghese were made by one of the greatest artists of the seventeenth century, Gian Lorenzo Bernini. Before we start visiting the museum, I would like to introduce you to this amazing artist. Now, Bernini is considered one of the best sculptors of the baroque style. In his lifetime, Bernini's contemporaries thought he was one of the most important artists that ever lived. However, this love for the man and his work has not always been this strong. Even Bernini himself knew that his reputation would worsen after his death, something he got right.

Only very recently has Bernini's reputation improved. After his death, the baroque style went out of fashion and Bernini's art was considered vulgar and exaggerated. In the last 150 years, art historians and critiques really disliked the work of Bernini. Fortunately, this period is over.

Today, we see Bernini for what he really was. He was one of the most influential and prolific artists of his day. His influence on the baroque style has been enormous. He has been an incredibly original artist and one of the few artists that still can touch you emotionally with his work.

Bernini was a true Uomo Universale, a universal man. This designation is often given to those artists from the Italian renaissance who seem to be able to do everything. Leonardo da Vinci was an amazing painter, but at the same time was thinking about the natural world in a way that was far beyond his own time. Michelangelo was a sculptor, but when he got the commission to paint the ceiling of the Sistine Chapel, he painted one of the most important works in Western painting. After, when he was appointed architect to Saint Peter's Basilica, he designed the famous dome of the church. Besides this, he was a good poet and his inventions in fortification helped defend Florence.

Bernini can easily stand in line with these incredible artists. Bernini not only sculpted statues, he put on shows, where he painted the scenery, carved the statues, invented the machines, composed the music, wrote the theater script and even built the theater.

Some of the comedies he wrote have been preserved and there are still some sketches by his hand for the staging of the theatre. There are even some sketches for the special effects and fireworks that Bernini wanted to use in these shows. Some sources say he painted hundreds of paintings.

However, nowadays we mostly admire Bernini for his work in sculpture and architecture, the two fields were he produced the greatest artworks.

Most of the art of Bernini can be found in the city of Rome. Bernini lived almost his whole life in Rome and it is for a large part thanks to him that Rome has a typical baroque character. His work can be found in Saint Peter's Basilica, where his designs adorn the most important places in the church. He sculpted saints, designed tombs, sculpted portraits of important cardinals, popes and noblemen. And let's not forget the many fountains by his hand that complete so many piazzas in Rome. Some of his most famous work can be found here, in the Galleria Borghese.

The Villa and Gardens

The building that houses the museum is also called The Casino. Casino is Italian for little house. It was designed by Scipio Borghese himself, who provided sketches to architect Flaminio Ponzio. After, the work was carried out by Giovanni Vasanzio. His name sounds very Italian, but his real name was Jan van Santen and he came from Holland. The Casino was built for Cardinal Scipio Borghese to provide a place for his collection of statues.

Once, the Casino was decorated with much more stucco and reliefs and also with ancient statues. However, a big part of the Borghese collection has been sold. Camillo Borghese was married to Pauline Bonaparte, Napoleon's sister. It seems Napoleon forced his brother-in-law to sell him part of the Borghese collection for a very low price. Nowadays, a big part of the collection resides in the Louvre, in Paris. Thanks to this sale, the ancient statues that decorated the façade of the Casino have disappeared.

When you are waiting outside to go in (you have to be at the museum to collect your tickets half an hour before you can go in), you might sit outside on the Balustrade that surrounded the entrance. This is a replica. The original Balustrade was taken out in 1982, when Paolo Borghese sold it to American billionaire William Waldorf Astor. Waldorf Astor used it to decorate his own villa in England.

After Napoleon bought many of the beautiful antique statues in the collection, Camillo Borghese and his descendants have bought other Roman statues to add to the collection. Furthermore, the painting collection of the Borghese family has been moved here and now occupies the first floor. Fortunately the art experts of Napoleon hated the art of Bernini, so they left Bernini's statues where they were.

The extensive park that surrounds the museum is confusingly called the Villa Borghese. When Romans talk about visiting the Villa

Borghese, they are talking about the park and not the Museum (something to keep in mind if you plan on going by taxi to the Museum). The museum is called Galleria Borghese and is located in the park Villa Borghese.

The park dates back to the time of Cardinal Scipio Borghese, who wanted to create a villa that was just like the ones Roman emperors used to have. The park was divided by the Casino. The part to the north of the Casino was the private part of the garden and the part to the south was public. There is still a small garden that is still private. This is the garden to the right of the main façade of the Casino. It is a citrus fruit orchard.

Today, the Villa Borghese park does not look like Scipio Borghese's park at all. Many changes have occurred throughout the centuries. It is a really nice place to walk around and a favorite of locals who go there in big numbers on sunny Sundays with their children and dogs. I would recommend taking a walk around after (or before) visiting the Galleria. Try to find your way to the viewpoint above Piazza del Popolo, where you have one of the best views of the city.

Part 1: Ground floor

Room 1: Pauline

Even though this room is not the room you enter the museum in, I always start a tour here. If you can, once you get into the museum, move directly to this room. Most people stop and admire the first main hall, but if you move to Room one, you will be with just a few people, unless you encounter me with a big tour group. The Galleria Borghese calls this Room also Room 1, so I guess it's the best place to start.

In the middle of this room you can see a statue by Antonio Canova. The statue portrays Pauline Borghese, who is more famous by her maiden name, Bonaparte. She was the sister of Napoleon, who married Camillo Borghese.

FIGURE 1 VENUS VICTRIX - ANTONIO CANOVA 1806

This statue shows you already a bit of Pauline's character. She wanted to be depicted as Venus, the goddess of love. It seems Canova first proposed to depict Pauline as Diana, goddess of the hunt. But when Pauline learned Diana had always stayed a virgin, she decided Venus would be more appropriate.

You can see she is supposed to be Venus, by the three apples in her hand. These apples are a symbol of Venus. When the Gods had dinner together on mount Olympus, the goddess of discord was never allowed to join them, for obvious reasons. She got angry and threw an apple at the table from the outside. Attached to the apple was a note, saying it was destined for the most beautiful Goddess. Of course three goddesses all thought they were most beautiful. To settle the dispute a young prince from Troy, Paris, was invited to be the judge. Venus, Juno and Minerva all promised Paris something if he chose them. Minerva promised Paris eternal wisdom. Juno promised Paris power over the world and Venus promised him the most beautiful girl in the world.

Of course Paris chose wrong and chose to have the most beautiful girl in the world. Venus won the competition and was allowed to keep the apple. The story does not end there though. The most beautiful woman in the world happened to be Helen, queen of Sparta. Paris went over there and kidnapped her, thus starting the Trojan war, which ended with his death and the destruction of his home city.

If you look up, you can see the same scene depicted on the ceiling, in a fresco by Domenico de Angelis from 1779.

Canova was a master of the neoclassical style. What does that mean? Around the time of the French revolution, artists became fed up with the excessive style of the Baroque and tried to go back to the basics. The basics in this case being the art of antiquity. The figures become less complicated and clearly adhere to the art ideals of antiquity. Look at the simplicity of Venus' pose here. When you will see the statues by Bernini in the next room, you can easily see that they stand in more complicated poses and in a way scream for attention. This is something completely different from this statue.

Pauline is portrayed in a simple and tranquil pose.

Canova sculpted this portrait between 1805 and 1808. It became quite a scandal when it was finished. Pauline showed herself almost naked to the world. You cannot see any drapery covering her. Only very few intimate friends of Camillo and Pauline were allowed to see the statue, and only by candlelight.

When people came to see it, a now lost mechanism in the wooden base was used that made the sculpture turn around.

Around Pauline you can see some superb statues from antiquity. Even though most people come here to see the statues by Bernini, Canova and some of the paintings, the collection of the Borghese family holds some amazing statues from antiquity. They all seem to be amazingly preserved, but do not be fooled. It was customary for noblemen to extensively restore classical statues once they bought them. If a statue was found without its legs or nose, a local artists was commissioned to provide a new nose, leg or hairdo.

Room 2: David

In Room two, your attention is immediately grabbed by the impressive work of art that stands in the middle. The statue depicts David, as he is in the process of throwing a stone at Goliath. David is an important subject in Italian art. Three of the most accomplished artists of all time all have made a statue of David and all are considered to be masterpieces with an enormous influence.

The first one was made by Donatello. It is very small and you can find it in the Bargello museum in Florence (a must see). It was the first nude depiction of a man in art after antiquity.

The second one everybody knows. Michelangelo's David is so well known that it even has become an icon of pop culture. You can buy mugs, shirts, posters and even 10.000 dollar real replicas in marble if you want to. Later I will make a comparison between this David and the David you see here, Bernini's David.

Bernini was born on the 7th of December in 1598 in Naples. His father was Neapolitan and his mother was a Florentine. Bernini moved with his family to Rome in 1605 and that is where Bernini would stay until his death in 1680. That is not a typo, he really lived to be 82, which was very old in that day of age.

In his long life, Bernini created an impressive body of artworks. Even for someone who lived to be 82, he produced so much work, that you almost cannot believe he did it in only 82 years. All these years he lived and worked in Rome, and that is why you really have to go to that city to see most of his work. Even though he was technically a Neapolitan, his life, art and person is closely connected to the eternal city. It was Bernini who shaped Rome the way we see it today.

One of the statues Bernini created, was a statue of David. Of course, the most famous David ever carved was the David by Michelangelo. Let's look at Michelangelo's David first, to examine the difference between the styles of the two masters.

FIGURE 2 MICHELANGELO, DAVID, 1501 - 1503

This is of course Michelangelo's David, one of the most famous statues in the world. This is a beautiful statue. David is standing quiet, watching Goliath in the distance. There is some tension in his body, which makes the statue come alive. The hands, feet and head seem a bit too big for his body. Many people say this was a mistake of Michelangelo, but this is far from the truth. This statue was meant to stand on top of the Duomo in Florence, very high up. To make the perspective fit, Michelangelo had to exaggerate his extremities.

David is very big, which some say is a symbol of Florence, a small city which is very big in aspirations and power. Of course, in the story David is small and Goliath is the big one.

Let's compare this masterpiece to Bernini's David, sculpted 121 years later.

FIGURE 3 BERNINI - DAVID, 1623

Bernini's David is very different, isn't it? David is not just waiting and looking at Goliath, he is right in the moment of swinging his stones at him. One millisecond later and Goliath is hit. Also look at the frown on his face. David is not relaxed at all, he is concentrating and doing his utmost to throw the stones as fast as he can. There is an enormous tension is his body. His toes are pressed against the floor and his eyes are fixed on his enemy. It is a very dramatic moment.

In this statue, you can see some characteristics of the Baroque. Just like with Pluto and Proserpina we see the moment that the action is happening. David is in the moment of throwing his stones with his sling. You can find another characteristic of the Baroque in the focus and composition of the statue. The whole statue is focused on Goliath, who is not sculpted of course. An imaginary Goliath stands in the room with us and David is completely focused on him. This makes us, as spectators, be much more involved in the statue. We are included in the action. We are standing on the battlefield and watching David defeating Goliath. This makes us part of the composition and it is something that makes this statue very different from the statues that came before it.

Some people say the face of David is the face of Bernini himself. The story goes that a visitor once saw him in front of the mirror making all sorts of strange faces. Only after seeing the statue of David complete did the visitor understand what Bernini had been doing. In fact, the face of David does resemble that of Bernini in this period.

This statue was commissioned by Cardinal Scipione Borghese. Bernini created it when he was 25 years old between 1623 and 1624.

Around the room you can see some beautiful reliefs from antiquity. Often tombs of important people were decorated this way and this art was very influential on artists of the renaissance and the baroque. Upstairs, where the painting collection is displayed, you will see some paintings by famous artists like Raphael, that were clearly inspired by this art. Often the reliefs on the tombs depict mythological scenes.

Room 3: Apollo and Daphne

In the next room you will find another statue that will you're your jaw drop. Bernini created this around the same time when he sculpted David. This is another of his masterpieces. It is actually amazing to think how many masterpieces Bernini created in such a short amount of time.

FIGURE 4 APOLLO AND DAPHNE, 1622

Here we see Daphne who is transforming into a laurel tree, to get away from Apollo. It is a true masterpiece. It is almost impossible to think that it was created using a single piece of marble. You can find this statue also in the Galleria Borghese.

The story goes as follows. Among other things, Apollo is the god of reason and he never lost his head. To teach him a lesson, Venus, the goddess of love and lust, sent Cupid to shoot two arrows. One arrow was made of gold and hit Apollo. The other one was made of lead and hit the nymph Daphne. This resulted in Apollo developing a very strong passion and love for Daphne. But at the same time, the lead arrow made all passion go away in Daphne.

Apollo cannot control himself and starts to run after Daphne, trying to take her by force. She really does not want Apollo to even touch her so she runs and begs the gods to help her. Her prayers are heard and she is transformed into a laurel tree, so Apollo cannot touch her. After this, Apollo starts to wear a laurel wreath around his head in memory of Daphne and the time he could not control himself.

Bernini manages to sculpt this story in an amazing way. He shows the moment of metamorphosis. Daphne is changing into a tree while we look. If you walk around the statue you can even see the metamorphosis happening. This is the first time anyone ever did this in sculpture.

Daphne is still very fearful. She looks back at Apollo, completely scared. She does not know what is happening yet. Apollo however is very much aware of the transformation that is taking place. This statue was made for Bernini's benefactor, Cardinal Scipione. He put them in his home.

Again, you can see some characteristics of the Baroque in this sculpture. Bernini sculpts the moment of action. The transformation of Daphne is happening while we look at it. Her hands are already turning into leaves and one leg is already made of wood.

Bernini creates a new style, but he does not forget to use his classical influences. For the face of Apollo he uses the same face of the Apollo Belvedere, a famous classical statue in the Vatican Museums. Michelangelo used the same face for his depiction of

Christ in his fresco of the Last Judgement in the Sistine Chapel. These artists create new forms of art, but are clearly inspired by the art of the Romans and the Greeks.

This statue has always stood in this villa. It might seem strange that such a pagan work was commissioned by a Cardinal. Many noblemen liked to have paintings or statues of pagan mythology in their home. It was very fashionable. Often, artists from the renaissance and the Baroque create a lot mythological work in the beginning of their career. They get their first commissions from the nobility. After, if they become more successful, they get more work from the church, the richest and most coveted employer. This is the case for artists as diverse as Bernini, Michelangelo (his Bacchus) and Botticelli (who went as far as to burn some of his own non-religious work during the religious extremism of Savonarola, in which he was caught up).

Scipione Borghese justified his possession of this statue by the inscription that you can see on the base. It is a small poem composed by his friend Maffeo Barberini, who later became Pope Urban VIII (and Bernini's greatest benefactor). The poem translates as: *Those who love to pursue fleeting forms of pleasure, in the end find only leaves and bitter berries in their hands.*

Room 4: The Emperors

After passing through the small chapel, you end up in the Room of the Emperors. In the middle you can see the statue of Pluto and Proserpina. Personally, I find this one of the most beautiful statues ever created by Bernini, and maybe even one of the most beautiful statues in the world.

FIGURE 5 PLUTO AND PROSERPINA, 1621

This statue is truly impressive. It is passionate and full of energy. It takes its subject from a classical myth, but the statue is far from classical. It looks completely different from Greek, Roman or even Renaissance statues. There is just so much more going on, so much more movement. It is beautiful.

The story that Bernini chose for this work of art is the myth of Pluto, the Roman and Greek god of the underworld and Proserpina, the daughter of Ceres, goddess of agriculture. Pluto grabs Proserpina, who is trying to get away from him.

Pluto is in need of a wife, because he feels all alone in the underworld, so he grabs Proserpina, while she was picking flowers. She was the daughter of the goddess of agriculture Ceres. Pluto abducts here and takes her to the underworld, where Proserpina becomes his wife. Ceres, her mother is devastated because of the loss of her daughter. She feels so bad that she starts roaming the earth, forgetting her tasks and burning every plant that comes in her way. Slowly, all plants start dying. Humans start dying too, because they cannot cultivate crops to eat. At that point Jupiter, the highest god, intervenes.

Jupiter does not have any problems with humans dying, the Roman gods are not so merciful. But what Jupiter does not like is the fact that humans are not able to sacrifice to the gods anymore. Therefore, he orders that Proserpina has to come back to the land of the living.

However, Pluto does not want his bride to leave so he gives her three pomegranate seeds to eat. Homer writes:

"But he on his part secretly gave her sweet pomegranate seed to eat, taking care for himself that she might not remain continually with grave, dark-robed Demeter."

When she came back above the ground her mother questioned her. Again, Homer writes:

"...but if you have tasted food, you must go back again beneath the secret places of the earth, there to dwell a third part of the seasons every year: yet for the two parts you shall be with me and the other deathless gods."

People and gods who eat something in the underworld are not allowed to leave the underworld. Because Proserpina just ate three little seeds, it was decided she would stay three months in the underworld, and the rest of the year she would spend with her mother.

This is the way the Greeks and Romans explained the seasons. Before Proserpina has to go to the underworld, her mother gets sad. All the plants start dying. This is autumn. Then in winter nothing grows. When Proserpina comes back after three months, everything starts to bloom again and spring starts.

The composition Bernini uses for his statue is a break with the past. In the statues he carved before this one, his style is mannerist. In this one, he transfers to the Baroque style that made him so famous. The composition of Mannerist statues often features a spiral movement, like in the statue in the image below, of Giambologna.

FIGURE 6 GIAMBOLOGNA, THE RAPE OF THE SABINE WOMEN, FLORENCE

This statue by Giambologna is truly mannerist. It represents the rape of the Sabine women. When Romulus founded Rome, he had a problem. The first inhabitants of Rome were all men. They were runaway slaves, pastors and criminals. Romulus realized he needed women for his city. Therefore, he invited a neighboring people, the

Sabines, for a festival. When they were all eating, Romulus made a sign with his sword and the Romans drew their swords and kidnapped the Sabine women. They retreated to Palatine hill, leaving the Sabine men without their daughters.

Giambologna captures this moment in his statue. A Sabine man looks up as a Roman takes his daughter away. Can you see the spiral movement in the statue? This is typical of the mannerist style. There is a lot of movement, but movement without reason. It is just esthetical movement.

By the way, before we return to Bernini, the story of the Sabine women did not end badly. The Sabine men were furious of course and returned to Rome with full armor and weapons. They laid siege to Rome, but before fighting could start, the Sabine women interfered. They stopped the war because they did not want to lose their fathers and new husbands on the same day. This is beautifully depicted by the neoclassical master Jacques-Louis David in this painting which hangs in the Louvre in Paris:

FIGURE 7 THE INTERVENTION OF THE SABINE WOMEN BY JACQUES-LOUIS DAVID, PARIS

The statue of Pluto and Proserpina can definitely be characterized as Baroque. Gone is the difficult spiral movement. It is a very emotional statue. Let's look at it again.

FIGURE 8 PLUTO AND PROSERPINA - DETAIL

Can you see there is a tear rolling down from Proserpina's cheek? It might be hard to see on a picture, but if you manage to go to the Galleria Borghese, you can see it clearly. This is really far from a classical or renaissance statue. Also, Pluto's hand presses deep into the flesh of Proserpina. She is very much made of flesh. There is a very big contrast between the softness and beauty of Proserpina's body and the hard and strong body of Pluto. There does not exist any classical statue that portrays a woman so sensual and soft.

You can also see one of the characteristics of the Baroque style. This is the fact that Bernini depicts a moment. It is the moment of action. Pluto (who is called Hades in Greek by the way) is right in the process of abducting Proserpina. She is screaming and fighting. It is the moment that is happening. You almost never see this in Renaissance, medieval or classical sculpture. It is an invention of Bernini. It makes the statue almost come alive. The figures do not seem to be captured in the stone. Instead they seem very much alive, fighting, struggling and sweating.

The statue of Pluto and Proserpina was created between 1621 and 1622. It did not stay long in Cardinal Scipione possession. After Bernini finished it, Scipione gave it to Cardinal Ludovisi. The statue stayed in this Cardinal's villa until 1908. In this year the Italian state bought it and returned it to the Villa Borghese.

This room is called the room of the emperors. This because you see a great collection of Imperial busts from antiquity all around the room. The busts look so new, almost like they were carved yesterday. Furthermore, the material used is porphyry, a very expensive kind of marble. Roman emperors loved to use this kind of marble, because of the purple color, which was the imperial color. In antiquity, it was only obtainable from one mine in Egypt.

Room 5: Hermaphrodite

This room houses a famous statue of a hermaphrodite.

FIGURE 9 THE ORIGNAL HERMAPHRODITUS, NOW IN THE LOUVRE

And blabla

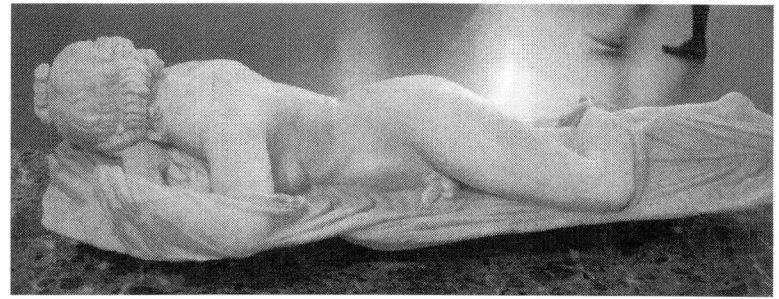

FIGURE 10 FRONT OF HERMAPHRODITUS - LOUVRE

The Sleeping Hermaphroditus is an ancient marble sculpture

depicting Hermaphroditus life size, reclining on a mattress sculpted by the Italian artist Gian Lorenzo Bernini in 1620. The form is partly derived from ancient portrayals of Venus and other female nudes, and partly from contemporaneous feminised Hellenistic portrayals of Dionysus/Bacchus. It represents a subject that was much repeated in Hellenistic times and in ancient Rome, to judge from the number of versions that have survived.

The ancient sculpture was discovered in the first decades of the seventeenth century—unearthed in the grounds of Santa Maria della Vittoria, near the Baths of Diocletian and within the bounds of the ancient Gardens of Sallust. The discovery was made either when the church foundations were being dug (in 1608) or when espaliers were being planted.

The sculpture was presented to the connoisseur, Cardinal Scipione Borghese, who in return granted the order the services of his architect Giovanni Battista Soria and paid for the façade of the church, albeit sixteen years later. In his new Villa Borghese, a room called the Room of the Hermaphrodite was devoted to it.

In 1620, Gian Lorenzo Bernini, Scipione's protégé, was paid sixty scudi for making the buttoned mattress upon which the Hermaphroditus reclines, so strikingly realistic that visitors are inclined to give it a testing prod.[4][5]

The sculpture was purchased in 1807 with many other pieces from the Borghese Collection, from principe Camillo Borghese, who had married Pauline Bonaparte, and was transferred to The Louvre,

Una copia risalente al II secolo è stata ritrovata nel 1781 ed ha in seguito preso il posto dell'originale all'interno della galleria Borghese.

Room 6: Aeneas and Anchises

When Bernini was very young, he created some statues in the style that was fashionable at the time, mannerism. The statue in this room shows Aeneas with his father Anchises on his shoulder.

FIGURE 11 AENEAS AND ANCHISES, 1618

Can you see the same spiral movement that also characterized Giambologna's statue that we saw before when we were looking at Pluto and Proserpina?

Mannerism is often called a reaction on the Renaissance style. Art and architecture in the Renaissance was often sober and harmonious. Mannerism is much more playful. Statues have complicated stances and dynamic movement. This is quite different from renaissance statues. This is the style Bernini sculpted in when he was young, but this did not last long. His statue of Aeneas is one of the last in mannerist style. Bernini then moves to the Baroque style, which he helped define.

But first, let's talk a bit about the statue of Aeneas. The story of Aeneas who flees from burning Troy is depicted very often in art. Aeneas was a Trojan hero who managed to flee from Troy when the Greek burned it to the ground. The Roman poet Virgil wrote a long epos about him. In this story Aeneas travels, just like Odysseus, all through the Mediterranean. He had many adventures, but eventually settles down in the area where later Rome was founded. Romulus and Remus, the mythological founders of Rome were descendants of Aeneas, and the Romans liked to think they descended from the Trojans and not the Greek.

This is why you often see Aeneas depicted, fleeing Troy, with his father Anchises on his shoulder and his son Ascanius next to him. It symbolizes the fact that Aeneas did not just escape from Troy, but he took his father, who represents his ancestors and culture, with him. This was important to the Romans, who liked to think they did descend from an ancient and important culture, but did not like to be associated to the Greek, who they admired in many ways, but also thought were unreliable and quick to quarrel.

Bernini sculpted the statue of Aeneas in 1618, when he was twenty years old. A few years later, he completed the sculpture of Pluto and Proserpina, in 1621. This means he made an enormous progression in just a few years.

In the same room, you can also see another statue by Bernini. Personally, I don't like this statue very much, possibly because it was never finished and looks incomplete.

In 1646 he started with a group of statues. The statue on the picture below is one part of it. Bernini never finished it.

FIGURE 12 TRUTH UNCOVERED, 1646

Bernini only managed to finish the statue of 'Truth'. The whole thing was supposed to be called 'Truth uncovered by Time'. We can see Truth depicted as a young, naked woman. Look at the veil, which is being pulled off her. The idea was that there would be another statue, representing Father Time, which would be in progress of unveiling the young woman symbolizing time. Truth is looking up, at the statue of Father Time, which was never made.

This group of statues was meant as a critique on the way the new Pope treated Bernini. The idea was that with time, the truth (Bernini's genius) would be revealed. Bernini was not wrong in this. The statue always stayed in Bernini's possession.

Another one of Bernini's very early sculptures can also be seen in this room.

FIGURE 13 ZEUS AND SATYR WHO ARE FED BY THE GOAT AMALTHEA, 1615

Bernini was only seventeen years old when he created this sculpture. It is no wonder Bernini started so early, because his father, Pietro Bernini also was a sculptor. His talents were much more modest than his son's though. Nevertheless, it was his father's support that got Bernini started in sculpture from a very early age.

Pietro worked in the Santa Maria Maggiore for Pope Paul V, when he arrived in Rome. He is also famous for creating the Fontana della Barcaccia, in front of the Spanish Steps. You can see Pietro was not an amazing sculptor when you see the fountain. It is nothing special, which is reflected in the name the Romans gave to it. Barca means boat in Italian and Barcaccia means something like ugly boat.

Pietro was quick to recognize his son's talents and told Pope Paul V about it. Paul V then referred the young Bernini to his nephew, Cardinal Scipio Borghese, who turned out to be a great benefactor to the young Bernini. From this moment, Bernini's career took off.

Room 7: Egyptian Room

This room has an Egyptian theme. It was designed by Antonio Asprucci in 1782, especially for the Egyptian statues that were in the Borghese collection. It was very common in these times to have at least some antique Egyptian statues in your collection. The Borghese family had a beautiful collection of Egyptian art, but unfortunately, most of it has been sold by Camilo Borghese to Napoleon and the collection has been dispersed all over Europe. What remains is the beautiful decoration of the room. The theme is 'The abundance of the Nile'. You can see this theme painted on the ceiling. The Nile, in the person of the man in the red cape, is flooding the valley, bringing life to Egypt. You can see crocodiles and lions and a sphinx in the background. The goddess standing next to the Nile is Cybele, the mother goddess.

Around the main fresco on the ceiling, you can see many smaller ones. These paintings represent the moon, Jupiter, Uranus, Saturn, Venus, Mars, the Sun and Mercury. On the walls you can see granite columns. It was thought at this time that granite was the favorite stone of the Egyptians.

Most of the room was emptied by Napoleon. Only the statue of the Gypsy Girl and two original oriental granite basins remain. The statues that you can see now in the room have been added later, such as the statue of a priestess of Isis, which did not come from Egypt, but which was made in ancient Rome. You can also see some sphinxes. They are not Egyptian either, but made by Romans. Romans really liked Egyptian art. For them, the Egyptian civilization was already 2000 years old, so they look to ancient Egypt like we look to ancient Rome. The Romans loved to take ancient Egyptian art from Egypt. Look at the many obelisks that you can see around Rome. They were almost all taken by the Romans from Egypt. There are now more ancient Egyptian Obelisks in Rome than there are in Egypt. But Romans also copied Egyptian statues, like the sphinxes you can see here. They even created their own obelisks, sometimes with meaningless hieroglyphs.

The hieroglyphs around the Egyptian room in the Galleria Borghese are fake too. They mean nothing. When they were painted, nobody knew how to decipher hieroglyps.

Room 8: Room of the Faun

Even though this room is named room of the Faun, the actual faun is not the most important work of art here. In this room you can find some of Caravaggio's masterpieces.

David with the head of Goliath

This is such an impressive painting. It is a great introduction to the artist Caravaggio. Caravaggio was not his real name. He was called Michelangelo Merisi, but maybe because the name Michelangelo was so much associated with Michelangelo Buonarotti, people called Michelangelo Merisi Caravaggio, because that was the town he came from.

In this painting you can see why Caravaggio was such an

important artist. Nobody was painting like him and nobody had painted like him. He was a major influence on later artists, from Velazquez to Rembrandt. While other artists, notably those from the Bolognese school like Domenichino and Carracci, painted opulent baroque paintings full of color, Caravaggio started painting these dark paintings in a style that had not been seen before. He did not have a great success during his lifetime, although he did attract a small group of noble supporters who loved his art. But the biggest art benefactor of the time, the church, did not give Caravaggio a lot of assignments. Maybe this was because Caravaggio liked to portray his saints as normal people from the street. Maybe because he used famous prostitutes as models for Mary or lower class alcoholics from the bars as models for saints.

As you would expect, he had a very colorful and dark life. At the beginning of his career he worked in Rome, but, in 1606, he had to flee, accused of murder. He had killed a man named Ranuccio Tomassoni in a street fight. A price was put on his head and Caravaggio fled. Two years later, he was thrown in jail in Malta, where he had joined the Knights of Malta. Why, we don't know, but he managed to escape from the jail and flee again, this time to Sicily. After, he made his way back to Naples. In fact, if you want to see some of Caravaggio's most famous works, you will have to go to these places yourself. There are some beautiful paintings in churches in Naples and in Syracuse in Sicily.

This painting was painted at the time of Caravaggio's run from the law. It depicts David with the head of Goliath. Goliath's head is a self-portrait of the artist, showing his emotional state during this time. He sent it to the Pope, looking for a Papal pardon, so he would be able to return to Rome. His pardon was finally granted, but the artist died on his way back to the eternal city.

The Madonna of the Palafrenieri

This painting caused Caravaggio quite some trouble. It was painted for Saint Peter's, but it was already removed after a month from the church. The authorities did not like it at all. Caravaggio did not paint it like he was supposed to. In this time, there were many conventions and rules that artists had to abide by, if they wanted to paint for the church.

However, this painting is beautiful. It shows Mary with baby Jesus and her mother Anna. Mary and Jesus crush evil and sin under their feet. Look at the dark light that Caravaggio shows his subjects in. Jesus and Mary seem to emanate light and bring light in darkness. If you look closer at the painting, you can see that the toenails of the subjects are dirty. You see this often in paintings by Caravaggio. He liked to show Saints and Jesus as normal people. They were not rich. They were not part of the nobility. Jesus came from a poor family and would have been just like you and me.

Another thing the church authorities did not like at all was the fact that Caravaggio had used a well-known prostitute as a model for his Mary. After the painting was removed, it came into the possession of Cardinal Scipio Borghese, who transferred it to the entrance hall of this building.

St. John the Baptist

This almost sensual painting of Saint John the Baptist is a very melancholic depiction of the saint. It seems Caravaggio has used a Roman street boy as a model. These days many people say Caravaggio was probably homosexual and we can see the same few boys reappearing in his paintings over and over again, often very sensually and almost erotically. This model was probably Mario Minitti, who you also can see here in the painting of the Boy with the basket of fruit.

Again, we see his toes and skin are dirty with dust. Saint John is not shown as a king or rich aristocrat or even as a godly figure. Caravaggio's saints are always very human, like he wants to show us that even we, poor human beings, can aspire to be saints. St. John was a normal boy, so a normal boy can become, if not a saint, than at least a moral and just person.

Boy with Basket of Fruit

This beautiful painting was stolen by the Borghese family. It belonged to the painter Giuseppe Cesari, better known as the Cavalier d'Arpino. He was one of the best known painters in Rome at that time and the young Caravaggio worked in his workshop when he just came to Rome. It was probably then when he painted this picture.

Cavalier d'Arpino had an enormous and famous collection of

paintings. The members of the Borghese family were also avid collectors and jealous of the collection. At this time, a member (Camillo Borghese, not to be confused with the husband of Pauline who sold big parts of the collection to Napoleon) of the Borghese family had been elected Pope. His nephew was Cardinal Scipio Borghese, a powerful figure himself. The Borghese family used their power to get their hands on the art collection of Cavalier d'Arpino. They fabricated some charges and had him thrown in prison. The Pope then confiscated his collection. Three of the Caravaggio's shown here are actually from the Cavalier d'Arpino, including this one: Boy with a Basket of Fruit.

The model was the same as the model he used for St. John, Mario Minniti from Sicily. He was Caravaggio's friend and companion and came from Syracuse, Sicily. When Caravaggio was on the run, Mario came with him to Syracuse, where he sheltered him and managed to get him a commission for a painting of Santa Lucia, the patron saint of the city. If you are ever in Syracuse, make sure to visit it.

The painting of the boy with the fruit shows off Caravaggio's skill with something as mundane as fruit. Some call Caravaggio the inventor of the still life.

Young Sick Bacchus

Here you see another self-portrait of Caravaggio. This time, he is not decapitated, but he portrays himself as a young and sick Bacchus, the god of wine. It was painted between 1593 and 1594, so right after Caravaggio came to Rome from Milan. Some physicians think when they look at the painting that Caravaggio was suffering from malaria, a common disease in Rome at that time. In fact, malaria is an Italian word. Mala means bad and Aria means air. The disease was thought to be the result from living in an area with bad air. People did not make the connection with the mosquitos yet. Some historical sources claim that Caravaggio was sick for six months.

This work also belonged to Cavalier d'Arpino and was confiscated by the Borghese Pope, Paul V. It is a beautiful painting. It clearly demonstrates the artists skill. Look at the skin of the sick Bacchus. You can see that he is sick. The fruit also shows off the skill of the artist. The skin of the grapes looks very realistic.

St. Jerome Writing

I love this painting because of the amazing way Saint Jerome's face is painted. It really looks like Caravaggio just got some old man from the streets, clothed him in a red robe and painted him like that. Look at the many wrinkles that adorn his face, his wild hair and the color on his face that must have been brought about by daily exposure to the sun.

Saint Jerome was a doctor of the Church who died in 420. He translated the bible into Latin. This version, the Vulgate, has been very influential. It allowed the Christian faith to spread much quicker.

The painting was painted during Caravaggio's late Roman period, which ended with his flight to Malta. It is very well possible that Caravaggio got the commission for this work from Scipio

Borghese himself. For a long time it was thought that it was painted by José Rivera also called Lo Spagnoletto (the little Spaniard). Rivera was a close follower of the style of Caravaggio and also loved to paint the rugged faces of old men, but art historians are now sure this is a real Caravaggio.

Entrance Hall

The entrance hall is quite impressive when you first enter the museum (unless it rained and you had to get in from inside). There are no really famous works of art here though. The most fun piece of art is the Roman mosaics that depict gladiators. These mosaics are antique and came were found on a Borghese estate at Torrenova, outside of Rome. You can see the gladiators performing all sorts of actions that would take place in the colosseum.

The fights of the gladiators were to most important part of a day at the Colosseum. These fights had a religious origin. Fights were organized at funerals. It was thought that the blood of prisoners could give deceased person strength on his trip to the underworld. But after a while these fights became very commercial. Rich magistrates would finance them to get support from the people. So after a few centuries the fights lost their religious context and became mass spectacles.

There were four schools for gladiators, which were called ludus in

Latin. They had space for 2000 gladiators each. The gladiators were well treated because they were very valuable. First most of them were slaves or prisoners of war, but later a lot of people volunteered. If you were poor and a good fighter you could become famous and rich by risking your life in the arena. Gladiators could be stars like modern athletes.

A day in the Colosseum would start with hunting games. Many animals from all over the empire and further away died in the Colosseum. When the Popes had the Colosseum cleaned and proclaimed a holy place, because of all the Christians that died there, a lot of very strange plants that did not grow in Italy were found. These came from the animal droppings. Many animals became extinct because of the Romans love for hunting games, like the North African elephant. When the Colosseum was opened in the year 80 during the reign of Emperor Titus, Vespasian's son, 900 wild animals were killed during 100 days. Below the arena there was a system of cages and cranes, which could make animals suddenly appear in the arena.

The other impressive piece of art in this entrance hall is the trompe l'oeil fresco on the ceiling. It was painted by Mariano Rossi from Sicily. He got the commission in 1774 from Prince Marcantonio IV Borghese. The scene he painted represents the apotheosis of Romulus, which means that Romulus becomes a god. He is taking his place amongst the gods on mount Olympus. Many scenes from Roman history can be seen, such as the victory of Roman hero Marcus Furius Camillus against the Gauls.

Part 2: First Floor

On the first floor of the museum, you can find the Borghese painting collection. The walls hang full with paintings from many different artists. This guide is not meant to give a complete description of all the pieces of art in the museum. Therefore, in this section I will show you the absolute highlights of the Borghese painting collection and I will skip those paintings that are lesser known. This does not mean they are not worth looking at, on the contrary. I invite you to look around and see what you like. When looking at Renaissance and Baroque painting it is very important to form your own opinions. Just look at the paintings and see if you like them. If you don't that is ok. Try to find out why you like certain paintings and why you dislike others. Enjoy your viewing!

The Deposition by Raphael

The first floor of the Galleria Borghese houses mostly paintings. I notice on my tours in the museum, that people are often much less impressed by the paintings here than with the statues downstairs. I can understand why. Renaissance paintings often do not have the immediate impact that a statue of Bernini can have.

I have to admit that I did not particularly like renaissance painting when I first started studying it. The problem with the paintings from this period is that they often depict religious scenes and often the same few ones over and over again. Much of this art was created for the church, which was the main benefactor of artists.

If you are already in love with renaissance art, bear with me for a while. I'm trying to explain to people who might not enjoy it as much, how to look at it. I only started enjoying this art after studying it and seeing many of the masterpieces in many museums in Italy. The trick is to truly look at the painting. Look at the faces. Look at the landscapes. And, most importantly, don't be afraid to judge. If you are in a museum with many paintings, like the galleria Borghese, don't be afraid to look around. Compare paintings. Why is one better than the other? What do you like about it? What don't you like? Compare the faces in one painting to the one next to it of another artist. Which one is better and why?

By asking yourself these questions, you will start to appreciate this art. Look for example at this painting by Raphael.

Raphael Sanzio is considered one of the best painters of the high renaissance and in this painting you can clearly see why. Look at the faces of the people. The painting is called Deposition. In it, you can see Christ after he is taken down from the cross. Look at the composition and really look at the people and the landscape, with Mount Golgotha in the background. Can you see how masterful this is painted? If you can't see it, look around you at some painting of a lesser known artist. You must be able to see the difference in quality.

This painting was painted for Atalanta Baglioni. She lost her son Grifonetto in a battle in Perugia and this painting was meant to remember him.

Do you remember the large Roman reliefs from sarcophagi you saw downstairs? These reliefs were very influential on artists from the renaissance. One of the characteristics of renaissance artists is that they try to use the art of Rome and Greece to improve their own art. Raphael had seen many of the reliefs in the sarcophagi and this painting is heavily influenced by this classical art form. He had seen some sarcophagi, where the mythological scene of the transportation of Meleager was depicted. Raphael recreated this scene, but this time with a Christian subject, the deposition of the cross.

After this painting was painted, it stayed in Perugia for many years, until it was stolen by a priest and sent to Pope Paul V, who gave it to his nephew. This is how the painting entered the collection of the Borghese family. It was once more stolen, this time by Napoleon in 1797 and was returned in 1816.

It is truly a beautiful piece and I can advise you to really take a bit of time to look at it.

Danaë by Correggio

Antonio Allegri was a painter from Correggio, a small town near Parma. Most people refer to him as Correggio, after the town he was from. This was not uncommon. Michelangelo Merisi is called Caravaggio, because he was from the town of Caravaggio.

Correggio is known as the most famous exponent of the Parma school of the Italian Renaissance. His contemporaries said he was a melancholic and introverted man. Not much is known about his early life. While his art was appreciated during his lifetime, centuries after his death, he became much more known and influential. Art lovers from the romantic period often wrote about his sensual work, full of soft tones, which appealed to the esthetics of the romantic period.

And these Romantic critics, tourists and art lovers were right. There is something in Correggio's work which seems far ahead of its time. Look at his Danäe. While it clearly resembles a renaissance work, it would be not too far-fetched to call it a Romantic painting.

This work is considered to be one of Correggio's masterpieces. The story of Danäe appears in the Roman poet Ovid's Metamorphoses (just like the story of Apollo and Daphne, which is so beautifully depicted by Bernini's statue). Danäe was the daughter of Arcrisius, the king of Argos. After the king heard a prophesy that he would be killed by her son, his grandson, he locked her up in a tower.

He did not know that Zeus, the first among gods, had set his eyes on her. Because Zeus was married, and his wife kept a close eye on him, he always had to transform, in order to sleep with a woman. In this case, he transformed himself into a golden rain.

In the painting you can see the golden rain falling on Danäe as she is being undressed by Cupid. Look at how sensual and soft this painting looks. The colors blend so nicely and the light seems to fall so gently on the soft white skin of Danäe.

Danäe became pregnant and gave birth to Perseus, the Greek hero, who did kill his grandfather, although by accident. At the foot of the bed you can see two small putti, who are testing gold and lead arrowheads.

The painting was commissioned by Federico II Gonzaga. After his death the painting changed hands (and countries) many times, until it was bought by Camillo Borghese in Paris.

Melissa by Dosso Dossi

    This painting is from a painter that is called Dosso Dossi. Just like before with Correggio, Dossi is not his actual last name, but the place he came from, San Giovanni del Dosso, a small village close to Mantua. Dossi is part of the Ferrara school of painting. For many years he worked for the Dukes of Ferrara, Alfonso I and Ercole II d'Este.

    Maybe you have heard the name d'Este before. Many people that visit Rome take the time to visit the Villa that the brother of Ercole II, Cardinal Ippolito d'Este has built, just outside of Rome, in Tivoli. If you have the time I can really recommend a day trip to

Tivoli to visit the Villa d'Este. The gardens are unique. I have never encountered anyone who has not been in awe of these gardens.

Let's look at this beautiful painting by Dossi. It actually comes from Ferrara and was sent by the Marquess Bentivoglio to Scipione Borghese around 1607 and this way entered the Borghese collection.

Look at the beautiful clothing of Melissa (it is however not completely clear who is painted in the painting, some say Melissa, some say Circe). Melissa was a nymph who discovered the use of honey. She was one of the nymphs who fed Zeus when he was a baby. You can see why art historians are confused by this painting: there are not a lot of references to this story in it. It was painted around 1530.

My guess is that it is a portrait of one of the ladies at the court of Ferrara, disguised as a mythological figure. This happened often during these days.

It is a truly beautiful painting, with soft light and colors and the beautifully dressed Melissa in the middle of the composition. Also notice the lush vegetation around her and the rustic village behind her.

The Last Supper by Jacobo Bassano

In this painting we see a scene that has often been depicted in religious art, the last supper. You must know Leonardo da Vinci's version of it in the refectory of the Convent of Santa Maria delle Grazie in Milan, which must be the most famous last supper ever painted.

Jacopo Bassano's Last Supper is clearly inspired by Leonardo's version, but Jacopo managed to make the scene his own. It is far less elegant and static. Here we see a scene that could very well have taken place in Bassano's own time. We see a group of people discussing and gesticulating during a meal. Look at the wrinkles that the hands on the table make in the tablecloth. Do you see the dog under the table? It is a beautiful composition, but Bassano clearly takes Leonardo's influence and creates something new and exciting. It seems that when you look at it, your eyes are carried around by the composition, exactly like Bassano intended. If you focus on one figure, he will lead you to the next and so on. It is very skillfully done.

The painting is one of the masterpieces of the sixteenth century. You see Christ, just as he is predicting that one of the apostles will betray him.

Bassano was an artist who was born near Venice. His paintings of simple country life became very popular in Venice, but in this painting he shows his true skill.

Diana and her Nymphs by Domenichino

I love this painting. There is just so much to see in it. Just look at the girl lying in the river at the foreground. She seems to look directly at you, involving you in the whole composition. The landscape is also very impressive, with clear a influence from the landscapes of Leonardo. You can see the mountains becoming more blue in the background. This is a natural phenomenon which you can easily notice yourself when driving or walking around through Italian hills.

The painter, Domenichino, was once considered to be one of the best painters that ever lived. His baroque art was seen as the high point of Italian baroque art. This all changed in 1840, when famous art historian John Ruskin launched his devastating attacks on the Bolognese school of painting, to which Domenichino belonged. Ruskin called Domenichino's art insincere and eclectic. This attack was so damning that not a lot of people, except art historians and people with an interest in the subject, have heard the name Domenichino.

These days we know better though. Even though the more dark baroque art of Caravaggio is much more popular in our time, there is no point in denying the power and skill of the painter Dominichino. And who knows, maybe in a hundred years a damning attack from another art historian will have people condemn Caravaggio and reembrace Domenichino.

In this painting of Diana, Domenichino uses a theme from antiquity, which makes a welcome diversion from most of his religious themed work, which sometimes can get a bit repetitive (in my humble view).

This scene is described in Virgil's Aeneid. Warriors are competing in an archery contest, shooting a tree, a ribbon and a bird. Domenichino changes the scene and places Diana, goddess of hunting, at the scene. I like this painting also because of the beautiful use of soft tones in the paint. He seems clearly inspired by the Venetian school of painting. Artists from Venice, like Bellini and Titian, almost always used these beautiful soft tones, a clear difference between them and artists like Michelangelo and Raphael, who used bright and strong colors.

Deposition by Peter Paul Rubens

When Pieter Paul Rubens came to stay in Rome, he painted this painting. It shows the deposition. Jesus is taken down from the cross and his dead body is being held up by his mother. What I like about this painting is the amazing depiction of the flesh of Christ. His flesh is white, but at the same time seems to emanate light. You can see the difference between the skin of Christ and the other figures most clearly if you look at the hand of Mary Magdalene, who holds his hand. Her hand is clearly alive and colored. The skillful blending of color of the flesh of Christ makes us understand his double nature. He is dead, but at the same time emanates light, foreshadowing his resurrection.

Also have a look at the altar Jesus is resting on. You can see clearly the influence Rubens visit to Rome had on him. It is a representation of an antique Roman altar with sacrificial scenes on it. The reliefs on these kinds of altars and tombs that were found everywhere around Rome were a great influence on many artists of the day. Remember how Raphael's Deposition that we saw before was also influenced by this kind of art? Many of the rooms downstairs in the Galleria Borghese are decorated by these kinds of reliefs.

Caravaggio's influence on Rubens can also be seen in this painting. Look at how dark the surroundings are and how beautifully the Godly light from above pierces this darkness. This is Rubens using Caravaggio and creating something new in his own personal style.

Another thing to look for in paintings by Rubens are the faces, especially of the women. He is very known for this particular and very characteristic style of painting women's faces. Their faces are always a bit white and blushing with often a beautiful expression of innocence.

The Concert by Gerard van Honthorst

This is a nice painting. The artist is not very well known, but people often remark this painting when they visit the Galleria Borghese. Maybe it is because it stands out between all the religious themed paintings in the collection. It was painted by a Dutch painter called Gerard van Honthorst who lived in the seventeenth century.

Van Honthorst moved to Italy around 1616 and perfected his art in Rome. He is part of a group of Dutch painters who were followers of Caravaggio. If you have seen the great paintings of the master himself in the Room of the Faun downstairs, you must recognize the clear influence Van Honthorst experienced from the work of Caravaggio. He lived for a while in a palace of an aristocratic family in Rome, where he saw a few Caravaggios in the families private collection. He got some important commissions from people like cardinal Barberini (later Pope Urban VIII) and Scipione Borghese, for whom he painted this painting.

Under the influence of Caravaggio, Van Honthorst specialized in night scenes with candlelight. These became very popular and earned him the nickname "Gherardo della Notte" or "Gerard of the Night"

In this painting you can easily determine the influence of Caravaggio. Besides the lighting of the scene, you can also see the basket of fruit on the table, something Caravaggio loved to paint.

Portrait of a Man by Antonello da Messina

Antonello da Messina is one of my favorite painters. He is not so well know, but his influence on the development of painting has been enormous. It seems Antonello visited Flanders at some point in his life and learned the technique of oil painting there. He then took this technique to Venice and introduced it to the local artists. This is how the Italians started using oil paint.

He was a Sicilian painter and to see some of his masterpieces you will have to travel there. There is a beautiful painting in the Mandralisca museum in Cefalù and another very famous one, the Virgin Annunciate in the Palazzo Abatellis in Palermo. Go, if you ever have the chance (not just for Antonello, but Sicily is a treasure trove in many respects).

I think Antonello is at his best when he paints a portrait, like in this painting here. Look at the strong individual character of the face. Look at the way the man looks at us. It is a beautiful portrait full of individual character, like many of Antonello's portraits. Can you see his red robe looks dirty? This is not the case, it is just that the lead based paint Antonello used for his highlights blackened over time.

Sacred and Profane Love by Titian

This painting is truly one of the masterpieces of the Borghese collection. It was painted by Titian when he was around twenty years old. It was commissioned to celebrate the marriage of Nicolò Aurelio from Venice and Laura Bagarotto. You can see Nicolò's coat of arms on the sarcophagus in the middle. He is not portrayed himself, just his bride on the left. Laura is assisted by Cupid and Venus. The bride, who has her hands on jewels, symbolizes the fleeting happiness that we can find on earth and Venus, with the burning flame of God's love in her hand, symbolizes the eternal love that can only be found in heaven.

Titian did not give this title to his painting. Sacred and Profane Love is a title given to the painting in the late eighteenth century. The title seems a bit moralistic, like it is saying earthly love is worse than heavenly love. This is not at all how Titian saw this painting. It was meant as a celebration of both kinds of love. Titian believed that you should contemplate the beauty of creation and enjoy it to understand the greatness of God, and this applied to earthly love as well.

You can see Titian comes from Venice in this painting. Venetian painters use much more soft tones in their art than their Roman and Florentine counterparts.

The painting is one of Titian's masterpieces. The rich Rotschild family liked the painting so much that they offered a price that was higher than the value of the whole Villa Borghese, including its artworks. Fortunately, it was not sold and you can still enjoy this beautiful painting in the Galleria Borghese.

Self Portrait by Gian Lorenzo Bernini

This painting was painted by Gian Lorenzo Bernini himself. Bernini is more known for his amazing statues and architecture, but as you can see, he was also a decent painter. You could say that Bernini was a true Uomo Universale. He knew how to paint, to sculpt, he designed architecture and fountains and he also wrote plays.

This painting is a self-portrait of Bernini in his younger years. I quite like it. It gives a good impression of the artist.

Part 3: Background

In this part you can read some background stories about the art of Bernini. I think these small background stories can be useful in understanding a bit more about the Baroque and the times Bernini lived in.

Urban VIII and Bernini's life

In 1623 something very important for the career of Bernini happened. Maffeo Barberini, a friend of Scipio Borghese, was elected Pope and took the name of Urban VIII. Contemporaries said he was a nice man with a friendly and open character. But he was also famous for his temperament and could get terribly angry all of a sudden. Like most Italians though, these spells of anger lasted not very long.

FIGURE 14 BERNINI - POPE URBAN VIII, 1630

Urban was a true fan of Bernini and decided to make good use of his talents. When he was elected Pope, he sent the following message to Bernini:

'It is your great fortune, sir, to get Maffeo Barberini as Pope, but we are much more fortunate to have mister Bernini live in the period of our Papacy'.

The Barberini Pope occupied the Papal throne for 23 years and all this time Bernini would work almost exclusively for the Pope and his family. The Pope loved Bernini and his work. This is the time when Bernini graduated from working with aristocrats such as Scipio Borghese and started working for the Church directly, a much more profitable benefactor. Urban VIII kept Bernini close and the artist became his trusted advisor on all things artistic. Many of the decisions that were taken in the Vatican at that time about construction, architecture, sculpture and painting were influenced by Bernini. The Pope treated him like a prince.

The Pope also recommended that Bernini marry. He did so, with a girl called Catherina. Together they raised four sons and five daughters. One of his sons, Domenico, wrote a biography about his father. In it he tells us that his father was loved by many. Bernini was a passionate man, but mostly used this passion in his art. When he was working, he often forgot where he was, the people around him and the time of day. He would say: 'leave me alone, I am in love'.

All sorts of people were allowed to visit his workplace, the poor and the rich alike. But everybody knew that they had to wait in absolute silence until Bernini was ready to receive them. This often resulted in people leaving without having talked to the artist, who was so captivated by his own work that he forgot everybody around him.

When Bernini was working, he worked seven hours a day. When Bernini was old, he told people that if you would add up the hours that he had not done anything, you would get no more than a month of time in total.

From Domenico, we also learn that Bernini was very critical of his own work. Once something was finished, he refused to see it ever again. This must have proven quite difficult at the end of his life, because he produced so much and many of it was in display in the most prominent places of the city he spent his life in, Rome.

One of the first commissions Bernini got under Pope Urban VIII was to create the Baldacchino in Saint Peter's, which he started in 1626. You can see how important it was for an artist of those days to get Papal commissions. The church was the most important sponsor of art. Most artists started out creating artworks for the aristocracy. Some never made the jump to working for the Pope, but those who did were sure to have a great career and make a lot of money.

Bernini's career went just like this. At first, he created statues for aristocratic families, like Apollo and Daphne and Pluto and Persephone. The aristocracy often liked these mythological themed art. Then, when his name was established, Bernini made the next move in his career and started working for the Pope. Now, he was able to create much bigger and important artworks.

The Baroque

Bernini himself was a faithful Catholic. Every morning he attended mass and every evening he would visit the Gesù, the first Jesuit church in Rome. He was a strong believer in the mission of the Jesuits. He also practiced the Exercitia Spiritualia. These are spiritual exercises that were created by the founder of the Jesuit order, Ignatius of Loyola. These exercises were designed to create religious feeling, by meditating and using your senses.

Bernini was most definitely a man of his time. The ideas of the Jesuits and the ideas of the counter-reformation influenced his art profoundly. If you look at the statue of David by Bernini, it is a typical baroque statue. It is very different from a renaissance statue. If we look at David by Michelangelo, we do not see a lot of emotion, especially compared to this David. Ancient statues never showed emotion. So this is something new. What is going on here?

This all goes back to a century earlier. In 1517 Luther nailed his 95 thesis on the church doors in Wittenberg and started the protestant reformation. This had a huge impact on the Catholic Church. Many Christians from the north stopped following the Catholic Church and became member of one of many protestant churches. At first, the Catholic Church was slow to react. But after a while it started to work to get people back to the (in their opinion) right church.

This went together with the fact that in 1492, Columbus had discovered America. Suddenly, the Catholic Church became aware that the world was a lot bigger than previously believed, and many of the people that lived in this world had never even heard of Jesus Christ.

So, by the beginning of the seventeenth century, the Catholic Church had decided it was time to get people back to the Church and to convert the people in Asia and America. Art was an important way of achieving this goal. And the Baroque was the style that was created to this end.

You have to remember, that when we look at the artworks and churches from this period, we might be amazed by the craft of the artist or architect, but the art had a completely different scope. This is something we often forget when we look at a baroque statue or church.

Basically, Baroque art is propaganda for the church.

You might ask, how is this propaganda? Nowadays, many people even berate the church for its opulent baroque churches, with their gold and marble decorations. 'How can you claim to take care of the poor, if your churches are so richly decorated?' people might say. In fact, people on my tours quite often ask this question. How can this rich and opulent art be propaganda?

To answer this question we have to look back at the statue of David. Luther had said that people had to read the Bible themselves. They should cultivate their direct relation with god. They did not need a priest for this. To this, the Catholic Church responded that many people did not know how to write or read the Bible. Many people in the new world had never even heard of the Bible and were absolutely not able to read it.

So, in order to get back the people that had left the church and to convert people that had never heard of Christ, the church started commissioning all these baroque statues. Through these statues, people would see what the Catholic faith could do to you. Look at the power David receives in the statue of Bernini. Look at his face. When a pilgrim would come to see this statue, he would understand what the faith could do with you. He or she could understand what true faith was and how it could make you feel. Indeed, feeling is very important in Baroque art and also in religious writing of the time.

Do you remember how Bernini would practice Ignatius of Loyola's spiritual exercises? These exercises were developed in the same time to get people emotionally involved in their faith.

Luther said read the Bible. But Catholics said, this is not enough. Just reading the Bible will not let you experience faith in the profound way that can truly influence and change a person.

Let's talk a bit about the term 'Baroque'. In Bernini's time nobody had heard of this term. It is only a word that has been given later to this style. Many of the labels people use in art history have a denigrating origin.

For example, the term 'Gothic', which designates a style of building and art from the middle ages that was mostly used in Northern Europe, comes from Italian art historians, who criticized this style. In the Renaissance, the Italians considered the Northern Gothic style as something from the northern barbarians. The goths were a people that once invaded Italy and were one of the reasons that the Western Roman Empire fell.

In the Renaissance, many of the progressive artists wanted to go back to the style of the Romans. They hated the style of the Cathedrals in France and called that style gothic.

The same thing happened with the Baroque style. Later art

historians thought this style was much too opulent and exaggerated. When the neoclassical style became prevalent in the 18th century, art historians started to use the Italian word 'barocco', which meant a difficult and complicated way of arguing, for the old style of the century before.

To truly understand the difference between Baroque and Renaissance, let's make a comparison. We all know (or should know) this statue:

FIGURE 15 MICHELANGELO, PIETÀ, 1499

This statue was made by Michelangelo in 1499. It is called 'La Pietà'. You can find in Saint Peter's in Rome. It is one of the most impressive statues ever made. It is a shame that is so hard to see in real life these days.

A modern vandal once broke parts of the statue and now it is protected by a strong glass wall. You cannot get close to it anymore, so you cannot see the immense beauty of the expressions of Jesus and Mary. Michelangelo was only 23 years old and it took him one year to sculpt. It is the only artwork by the artist that is signed. If you look at the ribbon across Maria's chest you can see his name. It says 'Michelangelo Buanorotte Florentino ha fatto questo', Michelangelo Buonarotti from Florence has made this.

He signed this work, because one day he was looking at his statue and some people came in and said the statue was made by a different sculptor. Michelangelo got angry and chiseled his name in at night. Michelangelo has been criticized for this work as well. Critics say that if Maria would stand up, she would be twice as big as Christ. Also, some considered Maria to be way too youthful. She looks younger than her son.

The reason Maria looks big, is because nowadays the statue stands in the wrong position. Michelangelo created it thinking it would stand on ground level. So you would look at the statue from above. If you look at the statue like that, suddenly the perspective works. The same applies to the David in Florence. People criticize this statue because its hands, feet and head are too big for its body. This is because the statue was meant to stand on the Cathedral, far up. People would only be able to see it from far, so he made the hands and feet bigger so you can notice them.

I show you this statue to compare it to a statue by Bernini. Michelangelo's statue is beautiful, but it is very private in a way. As a spectator, you feel like you are watching a very private moment. Mary is mourning her son. She takes him in her hands. You almost feel like a voyeur, looking at this scene. The statue is very sober, especially if you compare it to the other statues in Saint Peter's, which almost cry for attention. Most of these other statues are in the Baroque style.

Michelangelo's Pietà shows a very intimate scene. It is not made to woo you with exaggerated emotion. It is an intimate moment between a mother and her son. It is meant to make you contemplate life and death. In that sense, the statue is still a bit medieval. The execution is of course Renaissance, but the subject, death, comes from earlier times.

Let's compare this with one of Bernini's masterpieces.

FIGURE 16 SAINT THERESA OF AVILA, 1645

Here we see Saint Theresa of Avila. She was canonized in the seventeenth century. She is depicted in ecstasy. Theresa is one of three female doctors of the Church. She died in the night of the 4th to the 15th of October 1582. Incidentally, this was the night when a few days were skipped because of the introduction of the Gregorian calendar. She was canonized in 1622 and a few decades later Bernini designed the Cornaro chapel in the Santa Maria della Vittoria church to honor her.

The statue is made from one piece of marble. What is depicted in this scene? The religious writings of Theresa were very popular in this time. Who was this woman?

Theresa was born into a very religious and learned family from Spain. Recent research has shown that her family was a family of conversos. This Spanish word means 'converted ones'. Her ancestors were Jewish and lived in Toledo, at that time one of the most important cities in Spain, where people from three cultures lived together, the Jews, Christians and Arabs.

Then, in 1492, after the Catholic Kings conquered the last remaining stronghold of the Arabs, Granada, they decided they wanted all people in Spain to be Christian. People from other faiths had the choice to leave or to convert. Many Jews left and many others converted. Theresa's family converted. However, they still had to suffer a lot of discrimination in Toledo, and because they had some money, decided to buy an old aristocratic title and move city.

In Ávila, nobody knew they were once Jewish and after two generations, the family of Theresa was renowned for their faith. Some historians say that the family did keep some Jewish habits. The house Theresa grew up in was a learned house. Her father used to read her many books and she grew up to be quite knowledgeable.

The young Theresa was very religious and quite strong-willed. It is said, she once ran away from home to fight the moors when she was seven or eight. She soon returned, but this religious fervor would stay with her.

When she was older she became a nun and travelled throughout Castile barefoot, founding monasteries for the order of the Carmelitas Descalzas, the un-shoed Carmelites. Besides this, she wrote a lot of books about her spiritual awakening and her mysticism.

These books became very popular in the Rome of the Baroque period. The religious emotions that Theresa described in her books fit right in with the times.

Bernini chose one of the most famous passages of Theresa's books as a subject for his statue. Theresa famously got sometimes in some sort of trance, where angels talked to her. Theresa described this in one of her books like this:

'I saw an angel close by me, on my left side, in bodily form. This I am not accustomed to see, unless very rarely. Though I have visions of angels frequently, yet I see them only by an intellectual vision, such as I have spoken of before. It was our Lord's will that in this vision I should see the angel in this way. He was not large, but small of stature, and most beautiful — his face burning, as if he were one of the highest angels, who seem to be all of fire: they must be those whom we call cherubim. Their names they never tell me; but I see very well that there is in heaven so great a difference between one angel and another, and between these and the others, that I cannot explain it.

I saw in his hand a long spear of gold, and at the iron's point there seemed to be a little fire. He appeared to me to be thrusting it at times into my heart, and to pierce my very entrails; when he drew it out, he seemed to draw them out also, and to leave me all on fire with a great love of God. The pain was so great, that it made me moan; and yet so surpassing was the sweetness of this excessive pain, that I could not wish to be rid of it. The soul is satisfied now with nothing less than God. The pain is not bodily, but spiritual; though the body has its share in it, even a large one. It is a caressing of love so sweet which now takes place between the soul and God, that I pray God of His goodness to make him experience it who may think that I am lying.'

Bernini followed closely the description of the Saint, even in the slight erotic overtones of the description of her ecstasy. Theresa seems to float in the air and her face is looking ecstatic indeed.

Because of the erotic feeling of the statue, some people have argued to remove it from the Church or even destroy it. French author Charles de Brosses wrote in the 18th century: 'If this is heavenly love, then I know it very well'. Bernini himself considered this his masterpiece.

You must be able to see the difference between this statue and the Pietà by Michelangelo. Theresa seems to float. Her clothing seems to float too. Bernini clearly wants to show what emotions true faith can bring you. Don't we all want to experience religion like Theresa experiences it?

Theresa seems to experience pure joy, a joy that is even higher than what the physical world can bring you. Look at her face. She is completely captivated by her surrender to god. Her face points in the direction of heaven. Theresa is experiencing God directly. She is truly in ecstasy.

The scope of this statue is to captivate the spectator. Bernini wants you to experience the same profound and strong emotions Theresa is experiencing. In the Baroque the spectator is not just supposed to be a witness, like in the art of the renaissance and middle ages.

The art is supposed to stimulate you in the Baroque. You are invited to try to experience these kinds of strong religious emotions yourself. It is pure propaganda for the faith. Bernini does not just want to show you what once happened to Theresa, he wants to show you what enormous effect faith can have on you. He wants to show you what amazing feelings faith can give you.

This new way of looking at art started in the Counter-Reformation. The Catholic Church changed the way it used art. Before, art was just used to show and explain people stories from the Bible. Now, art had to convince people to believe. The church wanted to re-educate the Protestants and Catholics who had lost their way. The Church also wanted to convert all these new peoples that were discovered every day in the Asia, Africa and the America's.

Bernini created the statue of Theresa for the Cornaro chapel in the Santa Maria della Vittoria church in Rome. But, his commission was not just for the statue of Theresa, but for the whole chapel.

Bernini designed the chapel like a theatre. You can even see spectators in the tribunes. These are Cardinal Federico Cornaro and his ancestors. Bernini got the commission from a Venetian Cardinal Cornaro. He started in the year 1647. Bernini saw the chapel as a whole. Everything worked together. The statue and the architecture are one.

Take a look at the spectators in the tribunes.

This is a portrait of the person that gave Bernini the commission, the Cardinal from Venice. He is depicted together with his family members. Some seem to be reading, some seem to be discussing something. Art historians have fought long and hard over what these persons are talking about, but that is something we probably never find out.

Bernini was not the only one working in this new Baroque style. He was not the only one that wanted to show people what the faith could do with you if you believed and if you let yourself open to god.

If you are ever in Rome, make sure to visit the Sant'Ignazio church. This is the other Jesuit church in Rome. It is a beautiful Baroque church, which is very richly decorated. The church is most famous for the fresco painting on the ceiling. Let's have a look at this amazing work by the Jesuit monk Andrea Pozzo:

FIGURE 17 ANDREA POZZO, TRIUMPH OF SAINT IGNATIUS, 1685

It is an amazing example of perspective painting. If you stand on the marker in the middle of the nave of the church and look up, the perspective in the ceiling fresco is exactly right and the ceiling looks much higher than it actually is. But if you move to other parts of the church, the illusion is broken. You can try it by walking all the way to the altar and look back to the ceiling of the nave.

It is an amazing fresco and it was painted by a Jesuit monk, called Andrea Pozzo, who was also a mathematician. In it, he depicts the triumph of Saint Ignatius, the founder of the Jesuit order. Right in the middle of the fresco you can see Jesus, hanging on to his cross. From Jesus, a ray of light shoots towards Ignatius, who is sitting on a cloud. The light is then reflected by Ignatius and illuminates the four continents. These continents are reflected by the four pillars in the corners of the fresco. Their names are written on the pillars as well: Africa, Europe, Asia and America. Australia had not yet been discovered. The continents are also recognizable by symbols. A Native American can be seen around the American pillar and a black queen around the African.

What does this mean? Remember I told you the church was very aware of the fact that new peoples had been discovered (from a European perspective) and many of these people had never heard of Christ. The Jesuit order was an order which was very active in missionary work. In Pozzo's fresco, we see the light coming from Christ spreading across the four known continents, with Ignatius as the person who transmits the light.

Christ works through the Jesuit order to spread his light throughout the four continents. Remember that Australia had not been discovered at this time.

Then there is also the dome. The dome is not real, but also painted. The monks of the adjacent monastery did not want the big dome blocking the light in their library, so they asked the Jesuits to not build a dome. They did not build a dome, but instead asked

The Galleria Borghese

Andrea Pozzo to paint one. It is a gigantic trompe-l'oeil.

The church itself is a typical example of Roman baroque style. It is, of course, a Jesuit church and the baroque was a style the Jesuits often liked to use in their buildings.

When we see this ceiling today, we are amazed by the technical skill of Andrea Pozzo, but for us, the propagandistic nature of the work is much diminished. To truly understand the effect this work had in its time, we have to pretend to travel back in time.

Imagine you are a pilgrim, coming from a small town somewhere over the Alps. People did not travel very far in this time. There was no television, computer, or even picture books. This meant people generally had not seen many things. In a sense, we are very spoilt today. We can see the whole world by just looking up a picture or video on the internet. When we go to the movies we see can see things that are impossible, but have been brought to life with the special effects. We can travel by airplane and visit the whole world, and many of us have. No compare this to someone living in the seventeenth century. Communities were much more closed back then.

Some people chose to go on a pilgrimage to Rome, which could be a perilous adventure. They would walk for months and months and then finally they would arrive in Rome. Then, they would decide to visit the Sant'Ignazio church. Think about what they must have felt when they looked up and saw the ceiling. Imagine what effect it must have had on someone from a German or French provincial town. They would never have seen anything like it. Probably, they would not even understand how it was painted. They would not just believe that the painter was very good, but they must have believed he worked under godly inspiration. How could one man create such a magnificent work of art?

This was exactly the effect the Baroque artists tried to have with their art. They wanted to show the effect of godly inspiration. People should understand what true faith could do to a human being.

Sources

"Gian Lorenzo Bernini, self-portrait, c1623" by Gian Lorenzo Bernini - http://www.getty.edu/art/exhibitions/bernini/slideshow.html. Licensed under Public Domain via Wikimedia Commons - https://commons.wikimedia.org/wiki/File:Gian_Lorenzo_Bernini,_self-portrait,_c1623.jpg#/media/File:Gian_Lorenzo_Bernini,_self-portrait,_c1623.jpg

"ApolloAndDaphne" by Int3gr4te - Own work. Licensed under CC BY-SA 3.0 via Wikimedia Commons - https://commons.wikimedia.org/wiki/File:ApolloAndDaphne.JPG#/media/File:ApolloAndDaphne.JPG

"Rom, Santa Maria della Vittoria, Die Verzückung der Heiligen Theresa (Bernini)" by Dnalor 01 - Own work. Licensed under CC BY-SA 3.0 via Wikimedia Commons - https://commons.wikimedia.org/wiki/File:Rom,_Santa_Maria_della_Vittoria,_Die_Verz%C3%BCckung_der_Heiligen_Theresa_(Bernini).jpg#/media/File:Rom,_Santa_Maria_della_Vittoria,_Die_Verz%C3%BCckung_der_Heiligen_Theresa_(Bernini).jpg

"Blessed Ludovica Albertoni by Gian Lorenzo Bernini" by ho visto nina volare - Flickr. Licensed under CC BY-SA 2.0 via Wikimedia Commons - https://commons.wikimedia.org/wiki/File:Blessed_Ludovica_Albertoni_by_Gian_Lorenzo_Bernini.jpg#/media/File:Blessed_Ludovica_Albertoni_by_Gian_Lorenzo_Bernini.jpg

"The Rape of Proserpina 1 - Bernini - 1622 - Galleria Borghese, Rome". Licensed under Public Domain via Wikipedia - https://en.wikipedia.org/wiki/File:The_Rape_of_Proserpina_1_-_Bernini_-_1622_-_Galleria_Borghese,_Rome.jpg#/media/File:The_Rape_of_Proserpina_1_-_Bernini_-_1622_-_Galleria_Borghese,_Rome.jpg

"Bust of Pope Urban VIII by Bernini" by sailko - File:Gianlorenzo bernini, busto di urbano VIII 01.JPG (cropped). Licensed under CC BY-SA 3.0 via Wikimedia Commons - https://commons.wikimedia.org/wiki/File:Bust_of_Pope_Urban_VIII_by_Bernini.jpg#/media/File:Bust_of_Pope_Urban_VIII_by_Bernini.jpg

"Santa teresa di bernini 04" by I, Sailko. Licensed under CC BY 2.5 via Wikimedia Commons - https://commons.wikimedia.org/wiki/File:Santa_teresa_di_bernini_04.JPG#/media/File:Santa_teresa_di_bernini_04.JPG

"Bernini-goat with infants" by I, Peter80. Licensed under CC BY-SA 3.0 via Wikimedia Commons - https://commons.wikimedia.org/wiki/File:Bernini-goat_with_infants.JPG#/media/File:Bernini-goat_with_infants.JPG

"The Rape of Proserpina 2 - Bernini - 1622 - Galleria Borghese, Rome". Licensed under Public Domain via Wikipedia - https://en.wikipedia.org/wiki/File:The_Rape_of_Proserpina_2_-_Bernini_-_1622_-_Galleria_Borghese,_Rome.jpg#/media/File:The_Rape_of_Proserpina_2_-_Bernini_-_1622_-_Galleria_Borghese,_Rome.jpg

"Rape of Proserpina - Gian Lorenzo Bernini" by Int3gr4te - Own work. Licensed under CC BY-SA 3.0 via Wikimedia Commons - https://commons.wikimedia.org/wiki/File:Rape_of_Proserpina_-_Gian_Lorenzo_Bernini.jpg#/media/File:Rape_of_Proserpina_-_Gian_Lorenzo_Bernini.jpg

The Galleria Borghese

"Rapeofproserpinadetail" by Int3gr4te at the English language Wikipedia. Licensed under CC BY-SA 3.0 via Wikimedia Commons - https://commons.wikimedia.org/wiki/File:Rapeofproserpinadetail.JPG#/media/File:Rapeofproserpinadetail.JPG

"Bernini's David" by Galleria Borghese Official Site - http://galleriaborghese.beniculturali.it/. Licensed under CC BY-SA 4.0 via Wikimedia Commons - https://commons.wikimedia.org/wiki/File:Bernini%27s_David.jpg#/media/File:Bernini%27s_David.jpg

"Bernini Truth unveiled by Time Gal Borghese" by Gian Lorenzo Bernini - www.wga.hu. Licensed under Public Domain via Wikimedia Commons - https://commons.wikimedia.org/wiki/File:Bernini_Truth_unveiled_by_Time_Gal_Borghese.jpg#/media/File:Bernini_Truth_unveiled_by_Time_Gal_Borghese.jpg

"Santa teresa di bernini 03" by I, Sailko. Licensed under CC BY 2.5 via Wikimedia Commons - https://commons.wikimedia.org/wiki/File:Santa_teresa_di_bernini_03.JPG#/media/File:Santa_teresa_di_bernini_03.JPG

"Santa Maria della Vittoria - 1". Via Wikimedia Commons - https://commons.wikimedia.org/wiki/File:Santa_Maria_della_Vittoria_-_1.jpg#/media/File:Santa_Maria_della_Vittoria_-_1.jpg

"Cornaro SM della Vittoria" by Jastrow - Own work. Licensed under Public Domain via Wikimedia Commons - https://commons.wikimedia.org/wiki/File:Cornaro_SM_della_Vittoria.jpg#/media/File:Cornaro_SM_della_Vittoria.jpg

"Santa Maria della Vittoria - 6". Licensed under CC BY-SA 2.5 via Wikimedia Commons - https://commons.wikimedia.org/wiki/File:Santa_Maria_della_Vittoria_-_6.jpg#/media/File:Santa_Maria_della_Vittoria_-_6.jpg

"Michelangelo's Pieta 5450 cut out black" by Stanislav Traykov, Niabot (cut out) - Image:Michelangelo's Pieta 5450.jpg. Licensed under CC BY 2.5 via Wikimedia Commons - https://commons.wikimedia.org/wiki/File:Michelangelo%27s_Pieta_5450_cut_out_black.jpg#/media/File:Michelangelo%27s_Pieta_5450_cut_out_black.jpg

"David von Michelangelo" by Rico Heil (User:Silmaril) - private photo. Licensed under CC BY-SA 3.0 via Wikimedia Commons - https://commons.wikimedia.org/wiki/File:David_von_Michelangelo.jpg#/media/File:David_von_Michelangelo.jpg

"Giambologna raptodasabina" by Ricardo André Frantz (User:Tetraktys) - taken by Ricardo André Frantz. Licensed under CC BY-SA 3.0 via Wikimedia Commons media

"The Intervention of the Sabine Women" by Jacques-Louis David - Web Gallery of Art: Image Info about artwork. Licensed under Public Domain via Wikimedia Commons

ABOUT THE AUTHOR

Paul den Arend grew up in the Netherlands and has been travelling for most of his adult life. He studied art history in Salamanca, Spain, wrote reports for the Dutch Embassy in Santiago de Chile and studied Chinese in China. In between, he has been working as a tour guide. For many years he lived in Rome, Italy and guided groups of all backgrounds through the city. He has been a guide in the Vatican Museums, Saint Peter's and the Galleria Borghese, but he also loves to show groups around Sicily or Tuscany. His guidebooks reflect a profound love for the Eternal City and the many stories about its beautiful piazza's and landmarks.

Printed in Great Britain
by Amazon